333 WORD BOOK™
AROUND the NEIGHBORHOOD

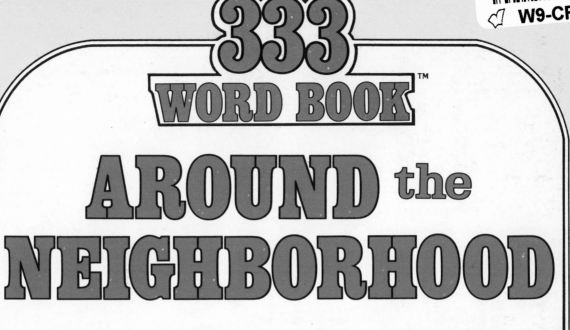

Illustrated by Robert Durham

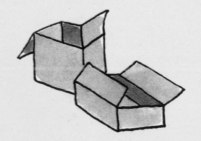

DERRYDALE BOOKS
New York

AT THE PARK

park
bench

water fountain

jump
rope

dog

cat

badminton net

thermos

jogger

birdie

helmet

gate

bushes

tree

radio

picnic table

picnic basket

badminton racket

picnic benches

jungle gym

skateboard

toy sailboat

pond

wagon

model airplane

rope ladder

ladder

slide

kite

cattails

kite tail

volleyball

roller skates

swings

pail

merry-go-round

butterfly

frog

horseshoe

sandbox

IN THE DEPARTMENT STORE

price tag

perfume

bicycle

football

bracelet

socks

ski poles

telephone

snorkel

scuba mask

air tanks

video cassette recorder

tricycle

watches

sneaker

television

skis

hockey stick

mirror

rings

earrings

doll

ice skate

hair spray

hockey puck

wig

telescope

necklace

toy truck

counter

salesclerk

computer terminal

toboggan

clocks

sled

hats

toy airplane

display case

basketball

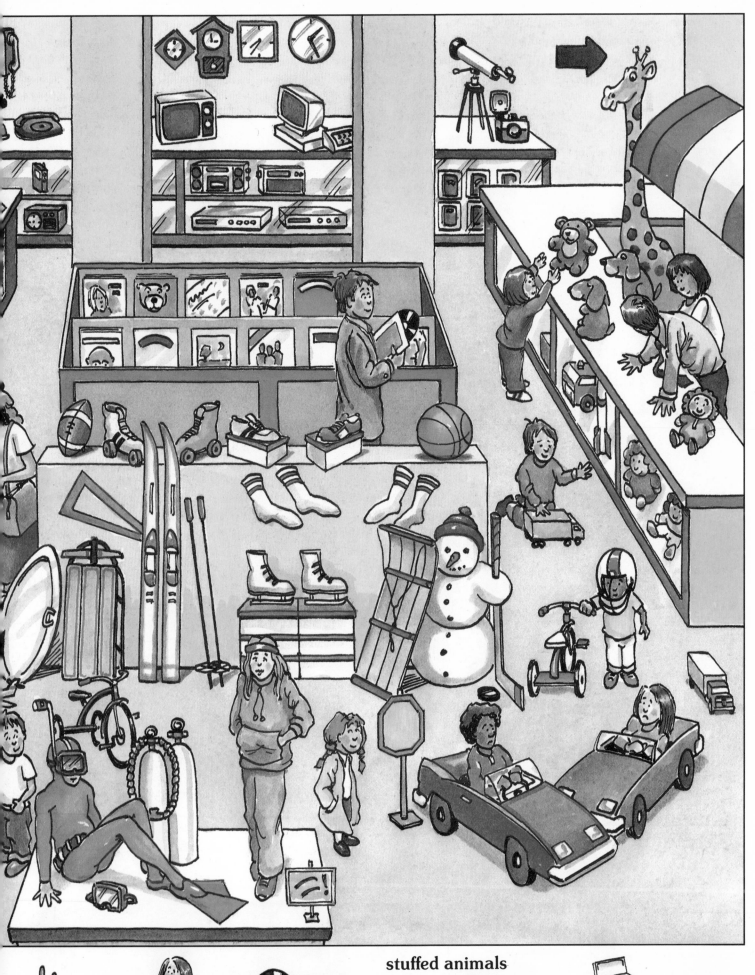

lipsticks

toy car

records

shoes

stuffed animals

eye makeup

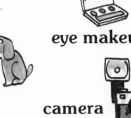
camera

ski hat

IN THE CLASSROOM

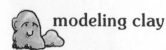 modeling clay

 headphones

tape recorder

 paste

drawings

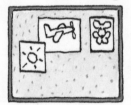

bulletin board

table

window

pencils

cage

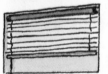

crayons   hamster

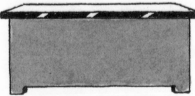

teacher's desk

paintbrushes

pencil sharpener

chair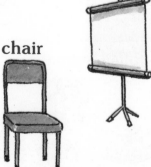

projection screen

blackboard

book bag

calendar

clock

painting

poster paint

easel

watercolors

alphabet

A B C D

bell

globe

apple

eraser

chalk

teacher

paper

record

record player

map

computer terminal

keyboard

slide projector

slides

ruler

bookcase

microscope

students

textbook

test tube

Bunsen burner

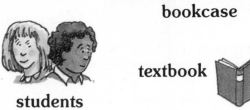

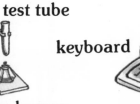

AT THE POOL

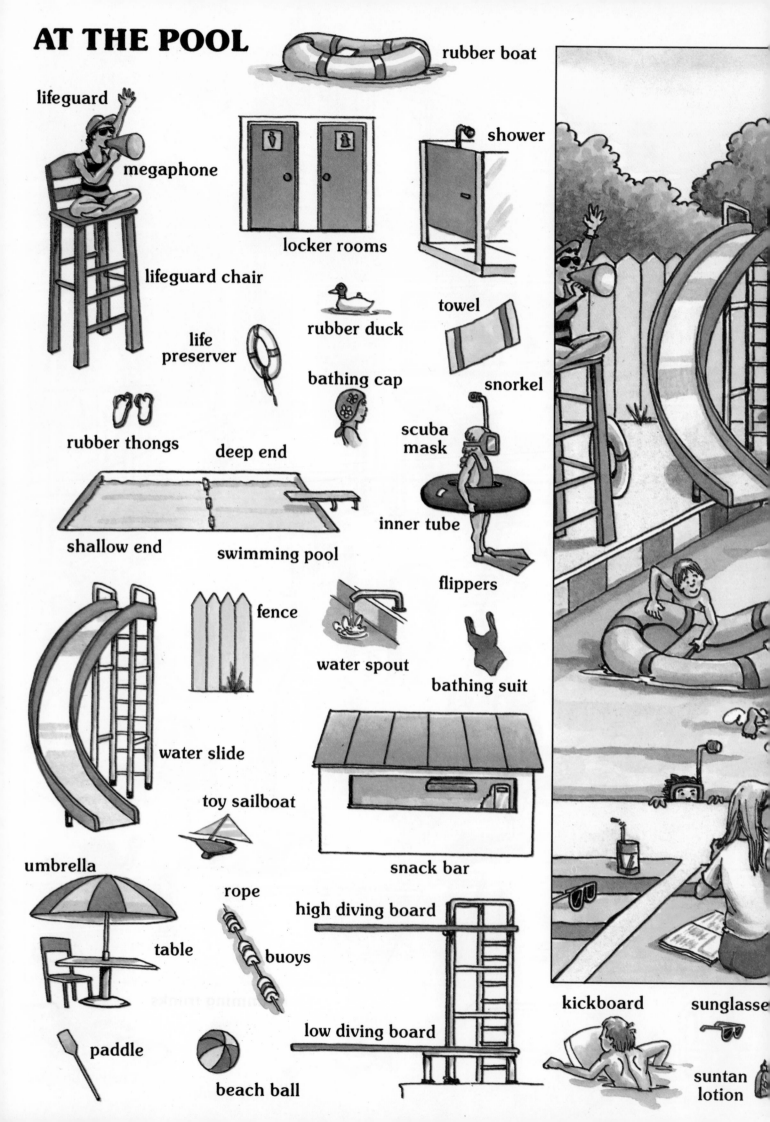

rubber boat

lifeguard

megaphone

shower

locker rooms

towel

lifeguard chair

rubber duck

life preserver

bathing cap

snorkel

scuba mask

rubber thongs

deep end

inner tube

shallow end

swimming pool

flippers

fence

water slide

water spout

bathing suit

toy sailboat

snack bar

umbrella

rope

high diving board

table

buoys

paddle

low diving board

beach ball

kickboard

sunglasses

suntan lotion

ladder **hot dog** **baby pool** **bikini** **swimming trunks** **soft drink** **chaise longue**

IN THE GROCERY STORE

sandwiches   bread

 sausage

 basket

 potatoes
eggplant

fish

apples

cash register

meat slicer

ham

bananas

check-out counter

cashier

grocery bag

boxes

gumball machines

chicken

cat food

carrots

pineapples

bottles

lobster

eggs

lettuce

scale

butcher

cucumbers

dog food

cans

milk

butter

meat cleaver

cantaloupes

grocery clerk

Swiss cheese

shopping cart

squash

broccoli

money

service bell

broom

orange juice

watermelon

AT THE MUSEUM

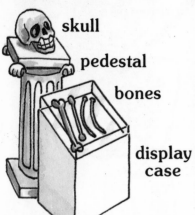
skull
pedestal
bones

display case

butterflies

walkie-talkie

security guard

shield

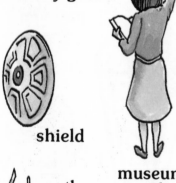
antlers

museum guide

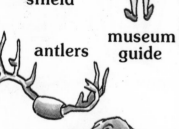
tyrannosaurus rex

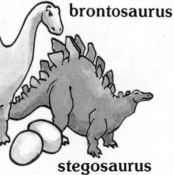
dinosaur eggs
brontosaurus
stegosaurus

suit of armor

headphones

tape player

sword

Roman soldier

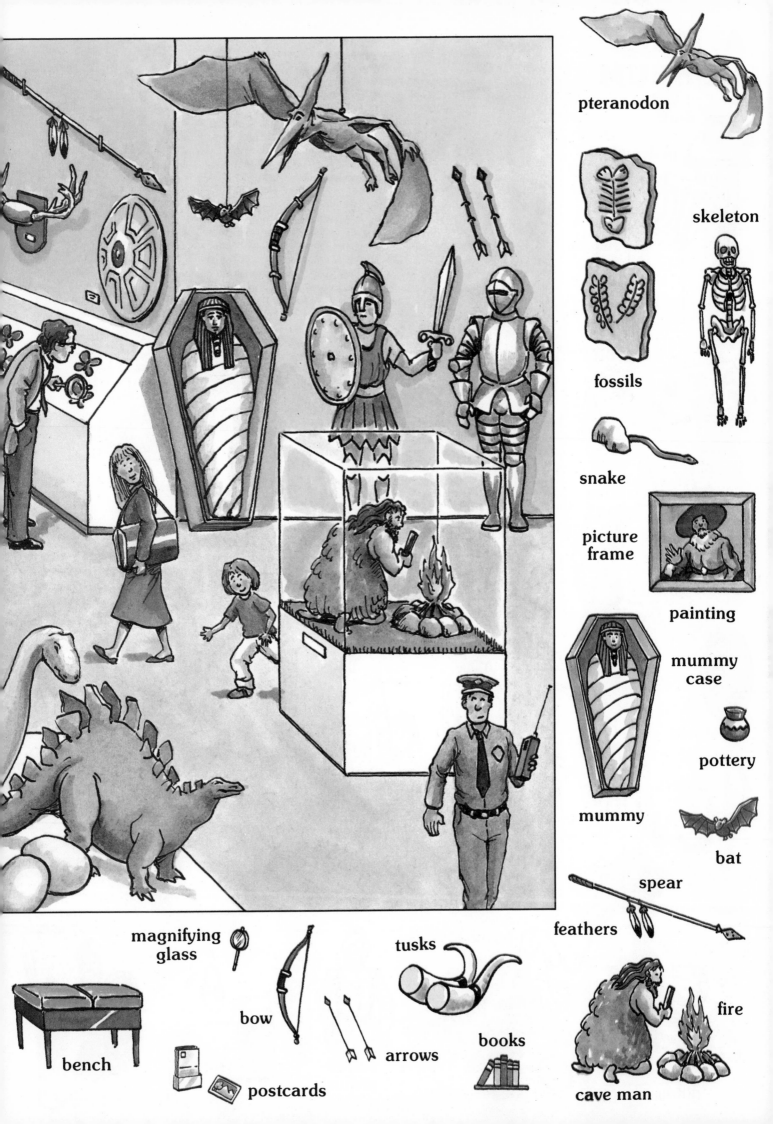

pteranodon

skeleton

fossils

snake

picture frame

painting

mummy case

pottery

mummy

bat

spear

feathers

fire

cave man

magnifying glass

tusks

bow

arrows

books

bench

postcards

IN THE HOSPITAL

patient

clipboard

x-rays

reflex hammer

oxygen tank

bed tray

flowers

get well card

examining table

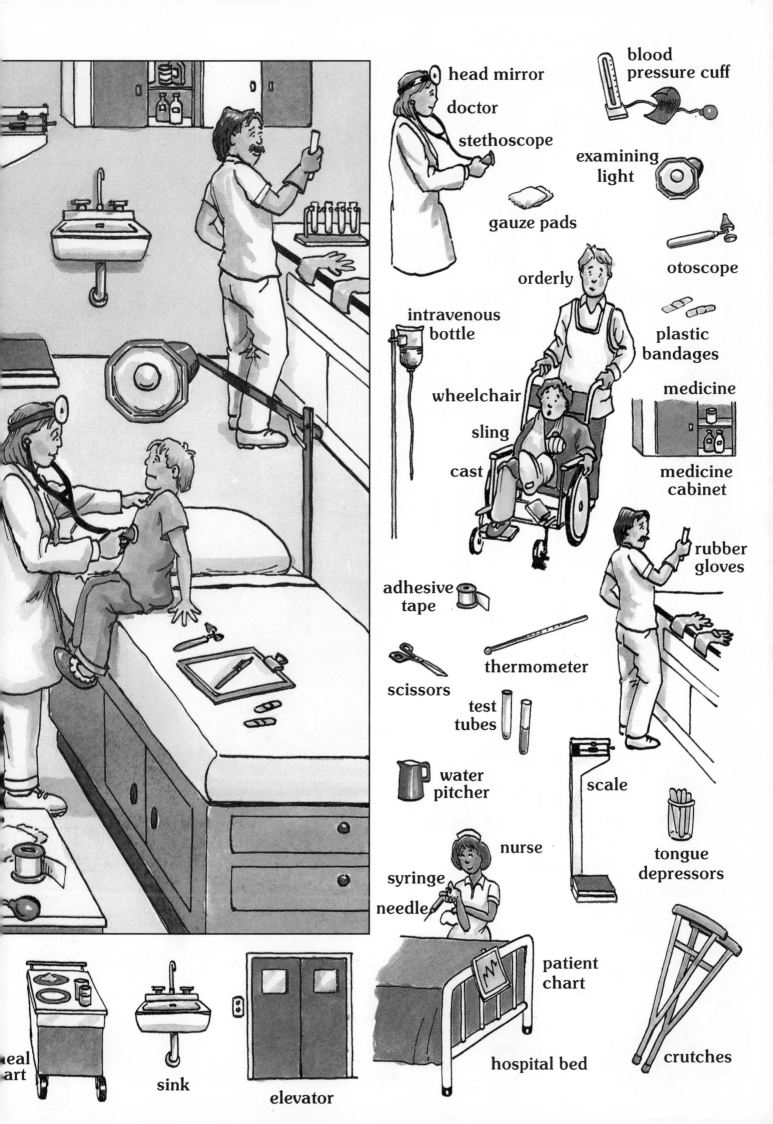

head mirror

doctor

stethoscope

blood pressure cuff

examining light

gauze pads

otoscope

orderly

intravenous bottle

plastic bandages

wheelchair

medicine

sling

cast

medicine cabinet

rubber gloves

adhesive tape

thermometer

scissors

test tubes

water pitcher

scale

nurse

tongue depressors

syringe

needle

patient chart

eal art

sink

elevator

hospital bed

crutches

ON MAIN STREET

drugstore

mailbox

manhole cover

manhole

barbershop

traffic policeman

clothing store

traffic light

street signs

public telephone

litter basket

road sign

streetlight

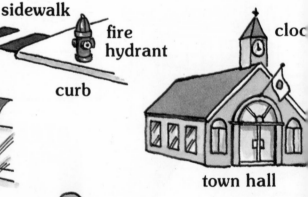

compressor

jackhammer

bus

sidewalk

crosswalk

fire hydrant

curb

clock

parking meter

bakery

town hall

billboard

car

service station

bus stop

dance studio

bookstore

skyscrap

gas pump

0 7 0 0 1

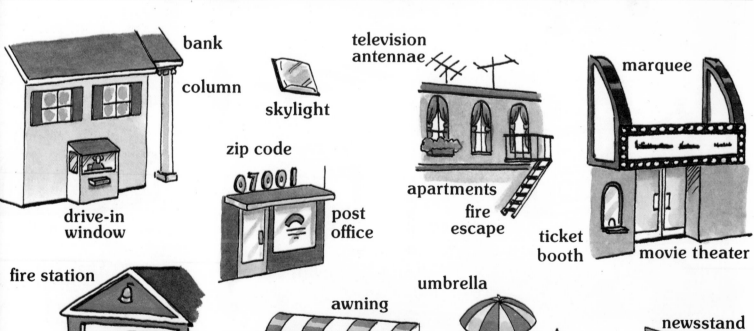

bank

column

skylight

television antennae

marquee

zip code

07001

post office

apartments

fire escape

ticket booth

movie theater

drive-in window

fire station

umbrella

awning

newsstand

fire engine

waiter

fire fighter

restaurant

outdoor cafe

AROUND THE NEIGHBORHOOD

A
adhesive tape
air tanks
alphabet
antlers
apartments
apples
arrows
awning

B
baby pool
badminton net
badminton racket
bakery
bananas
bandages
bank
barbershop
basket
basketball
bat
bathing cap
bathing suit
beach ball
bed tray
bell
bench
bicycle
bikini
billboard
birdie
blackboard
blood pressure cuff
bones
book bag
bookcase
books
bookstore
bottles
bow
boxes

bracelet
bread
broccoli
brontosaurus
broom
bulletin board
Bunsen burner
buoys
bus
bushes
bus stop
butcher
butter
butterflies
butterfly

C
cage
calendar
camera
cans
cantaloupes
car
carrots
cashier
cash register
cast
cat
cat food
cattails
cave man
chair
chaise lounge
chalk
check-out counter
chicken
clipboard
clocks
clothing store
column
compressor

computer terminal
counter
crayons
crosswalk
crutches
cucumbers
curb

D
dance studio
deep end
dinosaur eggs
display case
doctor
dog
dog food
doll
drawings
drive-in window
drugstore

E
earrings
easel
eggplant
eggs
elevator
eraser
examining light
examining table
eye makeup

F
feathers
fence
fire
fire engine
fire escape
fire fighter
fire hydrant
fire station
fish
flippers

WORD LIST

flowers
football
fossils
frog

G
gas pump
gate
gauze pads
get well card
globe
grocery bag
grocery clerk
gumball machines

H
hair spray
ham
hamster
hats
head mirror
headphones
helmet
high diving board
hockey puck
hockey stick
horseshoe
hospital bed
hot dog

I
ice skate
inner tube
intravenous bottle

J
jackhammer
jogger
jump rope
jungle gym

K
keyboard
kickboard
kite

kite tail

L
ladder
lettuce
lifeguard
lifeguard chair
life preserver
lipsticks
litter basket
lobster
locker rooms
low diving board

M
magnifying glass
mailbox
manhole
manhole cover
map
marquee
meal cart
meat cleaver
meat slicer
medicine
medicine cabinet
megaphone
merry-go-round
microscope
milk
mirror
model airplane
modeling clay
money
movie theater
mummy
mummy case
museum guide

N
necklace
needle
newsstand

nurse

O
orange juice
orderly
otoscope
outdoor cafe
oxygen tank

P
paddle
pail
paintbrushes
painting
paper
park bench
parking meter
paste
patient
patient chart
pedestal
pencils
pencil sharpener
perfume
picnic basket
picnic benches
picnic table
picture frame
pineapples
plastic bandages
pond
postcards
poster paint
post office
potatoes
pottery
price tag
projection screen
pteranodon
public telephone

R
radio

record player
records
reflex hammer
restaurant
rings
road sign
roller skates
Roman soldier
rope
rope ladder
rubber boat
rubber duck
rubber gloves
rubber thongs
ruler

S salesclerk
sandbox
sandwiches
sausage
scale
scissors
scuba mask
security guard
service bell
service station
shallow end
shield
shoes
shopping cart
shower
sidewalk
sink
skateboard
skeleton
ski hat
ski poles
skis
skull
skylight

skyscraper
sled
slide
slide projector
slides
sling
snack bar
snake
sneaker
snorkel
socks
soft drink
spear
squash
stegosaurus
stethoscope
streetlight
street signs
students
stuffed animals
suit of armor
sunglasses
suntan lotion
swimming pool
swimming trunks
swings
Swiss cheese
sword
syringe

T table
tape player
tape recorder
teacher
teacher's desk
telephone
telescope
television
television antennae
test tubes
textbook

thermometer
thermos
ticket booth
toboggan
tongue depressors
towel
town hall
toy airplane
toy car
toy sailboat
toy truck
traffic light
traffic policeman
tree
tricycle
tusks
tyrannosaurus rex

 umbrella

 video cassette
recorder
volleyball

 wagon
waiter
walkie-talkie
watches
watercolors
water fountain
watermelon
water pitcher
water slide
water spout
wheelchair
wig
window

X x-rays

 zip code